Lipizzans Are My Favorite!

Elaine Landau

LERNER PUBLICATIONS COMPANY • MINNEAPOLIS

Lerner Publications Company
A division of Lerner Publishing Group, Inc.
241 First Avenue North
Minneapolis, MN 55401 U.S.A.

Website address: www.lernerbooks.com

Library of Congress Cataloging-in-Publication Data

Landau, Elaine.
    Lipizzans are my favorite! / by Elaine Landau.
      p.   cm. — (My favorite horses)
    Includes index.
    ISBN 978-0-7613-6533-4 (lib. bdg. : alk. paper)
    1. Lipizzaner horse—Juvenile literature. I. Title.
  SF293.L5L36 2012
  636.1'38—dc22   2011011661

Manufactured in the United States of America
1 – PP – 12/31/11

PHOTO ACKNOWLEDGMENTS

The images in this book are used with the permission of: © Lynn Stone, pp. 3, 6, 7, 8 (both), 9, 10-11, 16, 17, 19 (bottom), 22; © Deepgreen/Dreamstime.com, p. 4; © Erich Lessing/Art Resource, NY, pp. 12, 13, 14; © Roland Schlager/EPA/CORBIS, p. 15; © Oriontrail/Shutterstock.com, p. 18; © Darlene Wohlart, pp. 19 (top), 21; © blickwinkel/Lenz/Alamy, p. 20.

Front Cover: © Tierfotoagentur/T. Musch/Alamy.
Back Cover: © Bob Langrish/Dorling Kindersley/Getty Images.

Main body text set in Atelier Sans ITC Std 16/24.
Typeface provided by International Typeface Corp.

TABLE OF CONTENTS

1443990

INTRODUCTION
YOUR DREAM HORSE

What's the horse of your dreams?

Do you long for a lively horse with a thick, flowing mane? Is a stunning white stallion up your alley? Sounds like you want a Lipizzan. These horses are known for their grace and good looks. Owning one would be a dream come true.

Unfortunately, the things we dream about don't always become reality. Have your parents said no to a horse? Perhaps the only pet they'll let you get is a turtle. Should you forget your horsey dreams and start reading up on reptiles? No way. You can still learn all about the Lipizzan. And who knows? Maybe someday when you're older, you'll own one after all!

Chapter One

MEET THE LIPIZZAN

The Lipizzan is a strikingly beautiful horse. It carries itself proudly. Even from a distance, you can tell it's special.

How Big Is That Horse?

A Lipizzan is about fifteen hands high at the highest part of its back. All horses are measured in hands. One hand is equal to 4 inches (10 centimeters). So a horse that is fifteen hands high is 60 inches (152 cm), or 5 feet (1.5 meters), tall.

Horsey Math

This equation shows about how high a Lipizzan is in inches and centimeters.

$$
\begin{array}{r}
15 \text{ hands} \\
\times\ 4 \text{ inches (10 cm)} \\
\hline
60 \text{ inches (152 cm)}
\end{array}
$$

A Lipizzan weighs around 1,300 pounds (590 kilograms). It's a light but sturdy horse. It has powerful shoulders and hindquarters and strong, muscular legs.

A Foal of a Different Color

Most adult **Lipizzans** are white. So it might surprise you to learn that **Lipizzan** foals aren't white when they are born. Newborn **Lipizzans** are often deep gray, brown, or blackish brown. Their coats lighten as they get older.

A Charming Personality

The Lipizzan's personality is as appealing as its looks. These horses are easygoing and gentle. Handling and training them is a joy. It's easy to fall for a Lipizzan!

Horse Diagram

You know that horses have a mane, a tail, and four hooves. But can you find a horse's hock? Or its forelock? Let's take a closer look at a horse. Soon you'll be an expert on all the parts that make up these fabulous animals.

back

croup

dock

flank

thigh

tail

barrel

hock

fetlock

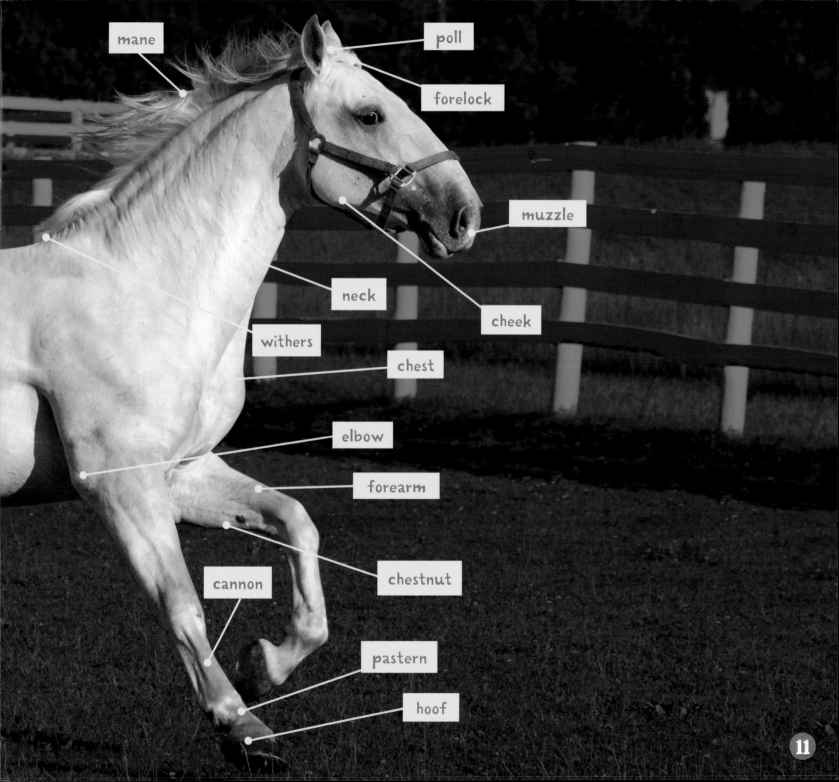

mane

poll

forelock

muzzle

neck

cheek

withers

chest

elbow

forearm

cannon

chestnut

pastern

hoof

Chapter Two

THE LIPIZZAN'S BEGINNINGS

The Lipizzan is one of the oldest horse breeds. These horses originally come from Spain. In the 1560s, Lipizzans spread to Austria. Austria's royal family loved Lipizzans, so they brought a large number of the horses to their country.

This drawing shows a Lipizzan performing in the 1700s in Austria.

An Austrian royal rides a Lipizzan in this painting of a celebration in the 1700s.

Different Uses

Some Lipizzans in Austria stayed in the royal stables. Others rode in parades. Still others served in battles.

The Spanish Riding School

A number of Lipizzans were sent to the Spanish Riding School. This school in Vienna, Austria, was created to train Lipizzans in dressage. That's a style of riding where a horse makes graceful movements in response to a rider's signals.

Rescue!

The Lipizzans in Austria almost died out during World War II (1939–1945). They were in danger from bombing raids. There was not enough food for them either. The head of the Spanish Riding School helped out. He moved the horses to Sankt Martin, an area in northern Austria. The U.S. Army took control of this region. It protected the horses until the war was over.

The Spanish Riding School still exists. People from around the world come to see Lipizzans perform dressage. Some say the horses look like a ballet troupe of four-footed dancers.

These days, Lipizzans can also be found in the United States. Lipizzans here often appear in circuses. They compete in horse shows. At times, they are used for trail riding or to pull carriages. No matter what type of work Lipizzans do, one thing is certain: these horses bring plenty of joy to the people around them.

Chapter Three

THE REAL DEAL

Would owning a Lipizzan *really* be great? Be careful what you wish for. Caring for a horse is a lot more work than having a turtle!

You can share your room with a brother or a sister. But you'll need to find another place for your horse. Do you live on a farm? If that's the case, your horse can stay in a fenced-in pasture. Your horse would also need a shelter of some sort. This could be a small, three-sided shelter to protect the horse in bad weather or on very hot days.

You'd be spending quite a bit of time in the pasture too. You'd have to feed and groom your horse. A Lipizzan's lovely coat must be kept clean. In addition, you'd need to clean up after your horse. Horses produce about 50 pounds (23 kg) of manure, or droppings, daily. So hold your nose and get a big shovel.

Stable Boarding

If you don't have extra land on hand, you can board your horse at a stable. There are different ways to do this. One is called full board. In this arrangement, your horse lives at the stable. People there care for it. That means less work for you. But full board costs quite a lot.

The other option is to have your horse live at the stable while you take care of it there. You'd need to go to the stable every day to feed, groom, and exercise your horse. You'd also have to shovel the manure out of its stall.

Taking Care of Tack

Horse owners do more than just care for their animals. They also wash their horse's saddle, reins, and other gear weekly. These items are known as tack. Tack should always be in tip-top shape.

Riding Styles

Did you know that there are two main styles of horseback riding? One style is known as English riding. The other style is called Western.

English riders (left) use English-style saddles. These saddles are lightweight and have a nearly flat seat. English riders hold the reins with both hands.

Western riders use Western-style saddles. Western saddles have a high front and back. They also have a horn. Western riders hold the reins with just one hand.

Move to the Groove

Humans can walk, skip, or run. Horses move in different ways too. These are called gaits.

Walking is the slowest gait. The horse lifts one foot at a time off the ground. **A** trot is the next fastest gait. The horse moves two of its legs forward at the same time. **A** canter is faster than a trot. The canter is a three-beat gait. **A** gallop is the fastest gait of all. **A** gallop feels like a very fast canter.

Horse Crazy

You don't have to own a horse to enjoy these animals.

Here are some other fun things you can do.

Make horses your hobby.

Find out all you can about the Lipizzan. Look for books, magazines, and movies they've been in. You might find YouTube videos about them too. Become a young expert on this breed.

Create a Lipizzan scrapbook.

Cut out pictures of these beautiful animals. The Internet has some great ones of Lipizzans performing. Jot down notes about their exciting shows. Pick out the horses you like best.

Get up close.

Many summer camps have horses. Maybe you can go to such a camp. Or ask your parents if you can take riding lessons. If riding lessons cost too much, see if you can do chores at a stable in return for free lessons.

Some summer camps offer horse lovers the chance to get up close with horses.

Lipizzans are truly great horses. Maybe someday you'll see them perform. Or maybe you'll just learn all about them. Either way, you'll enjoy getting to know these incredible animals.

GLOSSARY

breed: a particular type of horse. Horses of the same breed have the same body shape and general features.

dressage: a style of riding in which a horse makes graceful movements in response to a rider's signals

foal: a young horse

full board: an arrangement in which a horse owner pays staff at a stable to feed and care for the horse

gait: a word to describe a horse's movements. The four gaits are walk, trot, canter, and gallop.

groom: to brush and clean a horse

hand: a unit for measuring horses. One hand is equal to 4 inches (10 cm).

horn: a knob at the front of a Western-style saddle

tack: a horse's gear, including its saddle, reins, and bridle

FOR MORE INFORMATION

Brecke, Nicole, and Patricia M. Stockland. *Horses You Can Draw.* Minneapolis: Millbrook Press, 2010. Especially designed for horse lovers, this colorful book shows young readers how to draw different kinds of horses.

Horses—History for Kids!
http://www.historyforkids.org/learn/environment/horses.htm
Where did horses come from? When did people first start riding? Learn the answer to these and other questions at this interesting site.

Landau, Elaine. *Your Pet Pony.* New York: Children's Press, 2007. This is a good guide for young people on what it takes to own and care for a pony.

Lester, Alison. *Running with the Horses.* New York: NorthSouth, 2011. This dramatic story about ten-year-old Nina, her father, and their horses was inspired by the effort to rescue Austria's Lipizzans during World War II.

McDaniel, Lurlene. *A Horse for Mandy.* Minneapolis: Darby Creek, 2004. On her thirteenth birthday, Mandy gets her dream gift—a horse of her own. But will Mandy and her horse be able to save her best friend when tragedy strikes?

LERNER 🄴 SOURCE™
Expand learning beyond the printed book. Download free, complementary educational resources for this book from our website, www.lerneresource.com.

INDEX